Fire Risk The P

The Dutyholders' Shor   Risk:
Understand Requirements and Keep
People Safe Without Overspending,
Wasting Time or Going it Alone

Ian Stone and Neil Munro

Contents

Introduction

Welcome to "Fire Risk The Dark Arts: The Dutyholders' Shortcut to Fire Risk Assessments " a definitive resource designed to navigate the critical aspects of fire safety and risk management. In today's world, where the risk of fire in both commercial and residential settings is a significant concern, understanding and implementing effective fire safety practices is not just a regulatory requirement but a moral imperative. This book aims to equip readers with the knowledge and tools necessary to create safer environments in various settings.

The purpose of this book is to provide an in-depth exploration of fire risk assessments, an integral component of fire safety management. It serves as a crucial reference for business owners, safety professionals, risk assessors, and anyone responsible for fire safety within an organisation. Whether you are looking to refine existing fire safety practices or developing them from scratch, this book offers comprehensive insights into creating and maintaining effective fire safety protocols.

"Fire Risk The Dark Arts" is structured into several key sections, each addressing a specific area of fire risk assessment and management:

1. Understanding Fire Risk Assessment: This section lays the foundation, explaining what fire risk assessment is, its importance, and the legal frameworks governing it, particularly focusing on various international standards and practices.

2. Identifying and Evaluating Fire Hazards: Here, we delve into the practical aspects of identifying potential fire hazards in different environments and evaluating the associated risks.

3. Implementing Fire Safety Measures: This part discusses various preventive and mitigative strategies to minimise fire risks, including technological solutions and safety protocols.

4. Emergency Planning and Response: A critical aspect of fire safety, this section covers creating and implementing effective emergency evacuation plans and the role of training and drills.

5. Roles and Responsibilities: Emphasising the human element, this section outlines the responsibilities of duty holders, employees, and other stakeholders in maintaining fire safety.

6. Staying Updated: This section guides how to stay informed about evolving fire safety regulations and standards, an essential aspect of proactive risk management.

7. Case Studies and Real-World Applications: We present a series of case studies illustrating the application of fire risk assessment principles and the lessons learned from past incidents.

8. Glossary and Resources: The book concludes with a comprehensive glossary of terms and a list of useful resources and websites for further reading and reference.

Our approach in this book is to blend theoretical knowledge with practical application. The content is grounded in current research and best practices yet presented in a reader-friendly manner. We include illustrative diagrams, checklists, and real-life examples to enhance understanding and applicability.

"Fire Risk The Dark Arts" is more than just a guide; it's an essential tool in your fire safety toolkit. It is our hope that this book not only informs but also empowers you to take actionable steps towards ensuring fire safety in your environment, ultimately contributing to the wellbeing and security of communities and workplaces. Let's embark on this journey to a safer future, one where the risk of fire is acknowledged, understood, and effectively managed.

Who Are the Authors?

Ian Stone and Neil Munro are seasoned professionals in the UK health, safety, and compliance industry, with a company (Acorn Safety Services) that focuses on fire safety and risk management. As directors of Acorn Analytical Services and Acorn Safety Services, they have dedicated over two decades to helping companies navigate the complexities of health and safety regulations across the UK.

Their partnership extends over years, marked by a shared passion for safety and compliance, particularly in the realm of fire risk assessments. Ian and Neil's expertise, primarily honed in the field of asbestos management, has been enriched by their collaboration with numerous health and safety practitioners and fire safety specialists.

At Acorn Safety Services, Ian and Neil lead a dynamic team of fire safety experts, providing daily support to clients grappling with the intricate aspects of fire risk compliance.

This book is a culmination of their experience and insights, aiming to demystify fire risk assessments and enhance safety in businesses and public spaces. Their goal is straightforward – to make understanding and implementing fire risk assessments accessible to all and to prevent unnecessary exposure to fire hazards.

How To Use This Book?

Francis Bacon, the English essayist, once said, "Some books are to be tasted, others to be swallowed, and some few to be chewed and digested." This book caters to all types of readers. Whether you're a busy professional seeking quick information or someone who prefers a thorough, end-to-end read, this guide is designed to suit your needs.

Feel free to read it cover-to-cover, or dip into specific sections that pique your interest or meet your immediate requirements. It also serves as a handy reference tool for future use.

Each chapter concludes with a summary and actionable points, helping you gauge the section's relevance and decide if you need to delve deeper. Additionally, a brief overview at the end of each chapter contextualises the information and its practical application for duty holders.

The content is grounded in open-source information from the UK Government's Health and Safety Executive (HSE) and other reputable sources, ensuring reliability and relevance as of 2024. However, be mindful that some details may evolve with new findings or regulatory changes. The authors have taken great care to ensure accuracy and encourage readers to consult government and reliable sources for the latest updates.

The book is divided into various chapters, each with specific headings and subsections, covering various aspects of fire risk assessment. The final chapter offers a list of additional online resources, guiding you to further specific information on related subjects.

This guide will prove invaluable for anyone seeking comprehensive knowledge about fire risk assessment in non-domestic premises. It covers prevention, management, and control strategies to ensure a safe working environment, details on professional assistance for assessment and record-keeping, and insights into reviewing existing safety systems to prevent fire incidents.

Chapter 1:

What are fire risk assessments?

Fire risk assessments are systematic evaluations conducted to identify potential fire hazards in a building or workplace, determine the risk associated with these hazards, and implement measures to mitigate or eliminate the risks. The process involves five key steps:

1. **Identifying Fire Hazards**: Recognising potential sources of ignition, fuel, and oxygen in the premises.

2. **Determining Who is at Risk**: Assessing who could be harmed in the event of a fire, especially considering

vulnerable groups like the elderly, children, or those with disabilities.

3. **Evaluating Risks and Implementing Controls**: Analysing the likelihood and potential impact of a fire. Based on this evaluation, appropriate measures are put in place to reduce or eliminate fire hazards, such as installing fire alarms and ensuring clear evacuation routes.

4. **Recording Findings and Action Plans**: Documenting the hazards identified, the evaluation of the risks, and the measures implemented to address these risks. This step is crucial for legal compliance and future reference.

5. **Reviewing and Updating the Assessment**: Regularly reviewing the fire risk assessment to ensure it remains current, especially after any significant changes to the premises or its use.

The primary objective of a fire risk assessment is to ensure the safety of occupants and property, comply with legal fire safety regulations, and create a prepared and informed response in case of a fire emergency.

Chapter 2:

Who is a dutyholder?

In the context of fire risk assessments, a "dutyholder" is an individual or entity responsible for ensuring the safety of a building in terms of fire risk. This role is typically designated to:

- Employers: In a workplace, the employer is usually the dutyholder.

- Building Owners or Landlords: For residential buildings, the owner or landlord often takes on this role.

- Occupiers of a Building: In some cases, like in shared buildings, the occupier or tenant may have certain responsibilities.

- Facility or Building Managers: For large buildings or commercial properties a facilities or building manager might be appointed as the dutyholder.

Responsibilities of a Dutyholder

The dutyholder has several key responsibilities, including:

- Conducting Fire Risk Assessments: Regular assessments must be conducted to identify any potential fire hazards and risks.

- Implementing Safety Measures: Based on the assessment, appropriate fire safety measures should be put in place. This includes fire detection systems, fire-fighting equipment, and safe escape routes.

- Maintaining Documentation: Keeping records of fire risk assessments and any actions taken is crucial for compliance and future assessments.

- Ensuring Staff Training and Awareness: Staff should be trained on fire safety procedures and risks identified in the assessment.

- Regular Reviews and Updates: Fire risk assessments should be reviewed regularly and updated to reflect any changes in the building or occupancy.

Conducting a Fire Risk Assessment

A typical fire risk assessment involves several steps:

- Identifying Fire Hazards: This includes sources of ignition, fuel, and oxygen.

- Identifying People at Risk: Determining who may be at risk in the event of a fire, especially vulnerable individuals.

- Evaluating Risks and Implementing Measures: Assessing the likelihood and potential impact of a fire and implementing measures to mitigate these risks.

- Recording Findings and Implementing Them: Documenting the assessment and ensuring that the findings are implemented.

- Reviewing and Updating the Assessment: Regularly reviewing and updating the assessment to ensure it remains current.

Compliance and Legal Implications

Non-compliance with fire safety regulations can lead to severe legal implications, including fines and imprisonment. It's crucial for dutyholders to understand their responsibilities and ensure that they are adequately fulfilling them to protect the safety of occupants and comply with the law.

Chapter 3:

Understanding Fire Safety

Regulations

Understanding fire safety regulations in the UK is crucial for ensuring the safety and wellbeing of individuals in various types of buildings, whether they are residential, commercial, or public spaces. These regulations are primarily aimed at preventing fires and minimising the risks associated with them. Here's an overview:

Key Legislation

- The Regulatory Reform (Fire Safety) Order 2005 (RRFSO): This is the central piece of legislation in England and Wales. It applies to all non-domestic premises, including common parts of multi-occupied residential buildings.

- Fire (Scotland) Act 2005 and The Fire Safety (Scotland) Regulations 2006: These govern fire safety in Scotland.

- The Fire and Rescue Services (Northern Ireland) Order 2006 and The Fire Safety Regulations (Northern Ireland) 2010: Similar to the RRFSO, these apply in Northern Ireland.

General Principles

- Risk-Based Approach: The regulations adopt a risk-based approach, requiring the responsible person (dutyholder) to carry out a fire risk assessment.

- Responsibility: The dutyholder, who could be an employer, landlord, occupier, or building manager, is responsible for fire safety.

- Preventive and Protective Measures: The regulations mandate that appropriate fire safety measures are taken to prevent fires and protect people in case of fire.

Fire Risk Assessments

- Identification of Fire Hazards: Identifying potential sources of ignition, fuel, and oxygen.

- People at Risk: Determining who would be in danger in the event of a fire.

- Evaluate, Remove, or Reduce Risks: Evaluating the risks of a fire occurring and the risks to people from fire. Taking steps to remove or reduce fire hazards and risks.

- Record, Plan, and Train: Keeping records of the hazards and action plans, preparing an emergency plan, and providing training.

- Review and Update: Regularly reviewing and updating the risk assessment.

Compliance and Enforcement

- Local Fire and Rescue Authorities: They are the principal enforcing authorities for these regulations. They inspect premises, issue fire safety notices, and can prosecute if regulations are not complied with.

- Penalties for Non-compliance: Can include heavy fines and, in serious cases, imprisonment.

Fire Safety in Residential Buildings

1. Landlords and Building Owners: They must ensure that all fire safety measures are in place, especially in common areas of residential buildings.

2. Fire Safety in Individual Dwellings: While the RRFSO doesn't cover individual private dwellings, other legislation like housing standards and building regulations apply.

Fire Safety for Employers

1. Employers must ensure the safety of their employees and any other person on their premises. This includes conducting fire drills, providing fire safety information, and maintaining all fire safety equipment.

Special Considerations

1. High-Risk Buildings: Buildings like hospitals, schools, and high-rise buildings may have additional specific regulations due to their nature and the number of people they accommodate.

Understanding and adhering to fire safety regulations in the UK is not just a legal obligation but a crucial aspect of ensuring the safety and protection of individuals in various types of buildings. Regular fire risk assessments, appropriate preventive measures, and continuous review and updates are essential components of effective fire safety management.

Chapter 4:

The Regulatory Reform (Fire

Safety) Order 2005: An Overview

The Regulatory Reform (Fire Safety) Order 2005 (RRFSO), which came into effect in October 2006, is a significant piece of legislation in the United Kingdom that consolidates and rationalises the country's fire safety laws. It applies to England and Wales and represents a fundamental shift in the approach to fire safety. Here is a detailed explanation of its key aspects:

Purpose and Scope

1. Objective: The RRFSO aims to improve fire safety in all non-domestic premises, including workplaces, commercial buildings, and the communal areas of multi-occupied residential buildings.

2. Scope: It covers general fire precautions and other fire safety duties which are needed to protect 'relevant persons' in case of fire in and around most 'premises'.

Key Provisions

- Risk Assessment-Centric: The cornerstone of the RRFSO is the requirement for a 'responsible person' (usually the employer, occupier, or owner) to carry out a detailed fire risk assessment. This assessment must identify risks and hazards and be regularly reviewed.

- Elimination or Reduction of Risks: Based on the assessment, the responsible person must take appropriate measures to reduce or eliminate the risk of fire, as far as is reasonably practicable, and to ensure the safety of all occupants in case of fire.

- Fire Safety Arrangements: Implementation of appropriate fire safety arrangements, including fire detection and fighting equipment, emergency routes and exits, and maintenance of these provisions.

- Duty to Inform and Train: The responsible person must inform and train employees about the fire risks in the workplace and provide information to other relevant persons.

- Cooperation and Coordination: Where two or more responsible persons share premises, they must coordinate their fire safety efforts.

- Record Keeping: Keeping records of the risk assessment and subsequent actions is a critical requirement, especially for businesses with five or more employees.

Enforcement and Compliance

- Enforcement Authorities: The local fire and rescue authority is the primary enforcement agency. They conduct inspections, review fire risk assessments, and can issue notices.

- Enforcement Actions: These can include alteration notices, enforcement notices, and prohibition notices, depending on the nature and severity of the risk.

- Penalties for Non-compliance: Failure to comply can result in significant fines and, in extreme cases, imprisonment.

Impact on Fire Safety Management

- Shift to Self-Compliance: The RRFSO marked a shift from the traditional fire certificate system to a self-compliance system. It places the responsibility for fire safety squarely on the shoulders of the responsible person.

- Flexibility and Responsibility: The Order allows for a flexible approach to fire safety, tailored to the specific characteristics and use of the premises, but also demands a higher degree of responsibility from the duty holders.

The Regulatory Reform (Fire Safety) Order 2005 is an essential legal framework that guides fire safety management in non-domestic premises across England and Wales. Its emphasis on risk assessment, preventive measures, and the responsibility of the duty holders has significantly influenced the approach towards ensuring fire safety in various settings. Compliance with the RRFSO is not only a legal requirement but a crucial aspect of protecting lives and properties from the risk of fire.

Chapter 5:

Other Relevant Fire Safety

Regulations & Standards in the UK

In addition to The Regulatory Reform (Fire Safety) Order 2005 (RRFSO) in England and Wales, the UK has various other fire safety regulations and standards that apply across its different nations, as well as specific sectors and types of buildings. Understanding these is crucial for comprehensive fire safety management. Here's an overview of some of the key regulations and standards:

Scotland and Northern Ireland

- Fire (Scotland) Act 2005 and Fire Safety (Scotland) Regulations 2006: Similar to the RRFSO, these set out the duties for fire safety in non-domestic premises in Scotland, emphasising risk assessment and safety measures.

- The Fire and Rescue Services (Northern Ireland) Order 2006 and Fire Safety Regulations (Northern Ireland) 2010: These are the Northern Irish counterparts to the RRFSO, focusing on risk assessments and preventive measures.

Building Regulations

- Building Regulations (England and Wales, Scotland, Northern Ireland): These regulations include specific requirements for fire safety, known as Part B in England and Wales, Section 2 in Scotland, and Part E in Northern Ireland. They cover fire detection, alarm systems, fire resistance and spread of fire in buildings, means of escape, and access for firefighting.

- Approved Document B: Accompanying the Building Regulations, this provides guidance on how to comply with fire safety requirements in buildings.

Sector-Specific Regulations

- The Health and Safety at Work etc. Act 1974: This overarching legislation places a duty on employers to ensure the safety of their employees and the public. It encompasses fire safety as part of overall workplace safety.

- Management of Health and Safety at Work Regulations 1999: These regulations require employers to carry out risk assessments, which include fire safety risks.

- Housing Act 2004 (Housing Health and Safety Rating System): This applies to residential properties and assesses risks, including fire, in dwellings.

- Care Standards Act 2000: Applicable to care homes and similar establishments, mandating specific fire safety standards.

Standards and Guidance

1. British Standards (e.g., BS 5839): These are detailed standards for fire detection and alarm systems, fire extinguishing installations, and equipment.

2. Fire Safety Guidance Documents: Issued by government bodies, these provide detailed guidance on complying with the law in various types of buildings, like schools, hospitals, and care homes.

3. National Fire Safety Guidance (e.g., Fire Safety in Purpose-Built Flats, Fire Safety in the Home): These guidance documents are aimed at specific types of residential buildings, offering tailored advice for fire risk assessments and precautions.

Fire Safety in Specialised Buildings

1. Fire Safety in Healthcare Premises: Specific guidelines and codes of practice exist for healthcare facilities, focusing on the unique risks in these environments.

2. Educational Premises: There are specific guidelines for fire safety in schools, colleges, and universities, considering the unique layout and occupancy of these buildings.

In summary, fire safety regulations and standards in the UK encompass a broad range of areas, tailored to different types of premises and sectors. They ensure a comprehensive approach to fire safety, from building design and construction to everyday management of fire risks. Understanding and complying with these regulations and standards is essential for the safety of occupants and the legal compliance of businesses and other organisations.

Chapter 6:

Changes in Fire Safety Regulations

Over the Years in the UK

The landscape of fire safety regulations in the UK has undergone significant changes over the years, evolving in response to emerging risks, technological advancements, and lessons learned from major fire incidents. Here's an overview of how these regulations have changed:

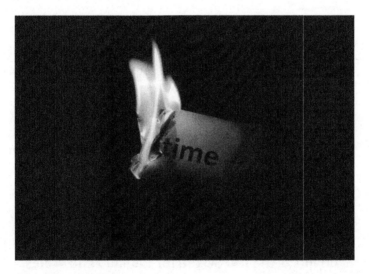

Post-War to the 1970s

1. Fire Precautions Act 1971: This was one of the early comprehensive pieces of legislation. It required fire certificates for certain types of buildings and established basic fire safety requirements.

2. Health and Safety at Work etc. Act 1974: While not exclusively about fire safety, this Act imposed general duties on employers to ensure the safety of employees and the public, which included fire safety measures.

1980s and 1990s

1. Fire Safety and Safety of Places of Sport Act 1987: Following the Bradford City stadium fire, this Act introduced safety certificates for sports grounds.

2. Building Regulations: Throughout the 1980s and 1990s, there were periodic updates to the Building Regulations, particularly Part B, which deals with fire safety. These updates reflected new building practices and materials, emphasising the importance of fire-resistant materials and the design of escape routes.

Early 2000s

1. Regulatory Reform (Fire Safety) Order 2005 (RRFSO): This was a landmark change in fire safety legislation in England and Wales. It replaced over 70 pieces of fire safety law, including the Fire Precautions Act 1971 and the fire aspects of the Health and Safety at Work Act. The RRFSO shifted the focus to a risk-based approach, requiring responsible persons to conduct fire risk assessments and implement appropriate safety measures.

2. Fire (Scotland) Act 2005 and Fire Safety (Scotland) Regulations 2006: These established similar principles in Scotland as the RRFSO did for England and Wales.

3. The Fire and Rescue Services (Northern Ireland) Order 2006 and Fire Safety Regulations (Northern Ireland) 2010: Similar to the RRFSO, these were implemented in Northern Ireland.

Post-2000s Developments

1. Grenfell Tower Fire 2017: This tragic event, where 72 people lost their lives, led to a re-evaluation of fire safety regulations, particularly concerning high-rise residential buildings. It highlighted issues such as the use of combustible cladding materials and the 'stay put' policy.

2. Building Safety Bill 2021: Introduced in response to the Grenfell Tower inquiry, this bill aims to improve building and fire safety in high-rise residential buildings. Key proposals include establishing a new Building Safety Regulator, enhancing residents' rights, and stronger oversight over the safety of construction products.

3. Hackitt Review: An independent review of building regulations and fire safety, led by Dame Judith Hackitt, called for a "radical rethink" of the regulatory system. The review recommended a more rigorous approach to fire safety in high-rise residential buildings.

Over the years, the evolution of fire safety regulations in the UK reflects a growing understanding of fire risks and the need for a proactive, comprehensive approach to fire safety. From prescriptive rules to a more risk-based, holistic strategy, these changes underscore the commitment to preventing fire incidents and protecting lives and properties. The continuous review and updating of these regulations, especially in the wake of major fire incidents, demonstrate the dynamic nature of fire safety management and the need for ongoing vigilance and improvement.

Chapter 7:

Who Is Responsible for Fire Safety?

In the United Kingdom, the responsibility for fire safety in buildings, particularly in the context of workplaces and non-domestic premises, is clearly defined under various fire safety regulations. The key concept introduced by these regulations is that of the 'responsible person'. Here's a detailed look at who this entails:

The Responsible Person

1. Definition: The 'responsible person' is defined primarily in the Regulatory Reform (Fire Safety) Order 2005 for England and Wales, with similar definitions in corresponding legislation in Scotland and Northern Ireland. This is typically the individual or entity who has control over premises or certain areas within premises.

2. In Workplaces: The employer is usually the responsible person in a workplace. If there's more than one employer, each one is responsible for compliance in relation to their work activity.

3. In Shared Buildings: In buildings with multiple occupants, such as shared office buildings or multi-occupancy residential buildings, the responsibility can be shared. Landlords, managing agents, or owners of the building might be responsible for common areas, while individual business owners or tenants are responsible for the areas they occupy.

4. For Landlords and Building Owners: Landlords or building owners are responsible for fire safety in communal areas of residential buildings and must ensure the building complies with regulations.

Responsibilities of the Responsible Person

1. Conducting Fire Risk Assessments: Carrying out a comprehensive fire risk assessment to identify potential fire hazards and risks.

2. Implementing and Maintaining Fire Safety Measures: Based on the risk assessment, implementing appropriate fire safety measures, such as fire alarms, extinguishers, and emergency lighting, and maintaining them in good working order.

3. Creating Emergency Plans: Developing and maintaining a clear fire safety and evacuation plan, tailored to the specific characteristics of the premises.

4. Providing Information and Training: Ensuring that all employees or residents are informed about the risks and

the fire safety procedures in place. This includes regular fire safety training and drills.

5. Working with Other Responsible Persons: In shared premises, coordinating fire safety practices and sharing relevant information with others who have fire safety responsibilities.

6. Compliance with Regulations: Ensuring compliance with all relevant fire safety regulations, including keeping up to date with any changes in legislation.

Shared Responsibility

In many cases, fire safety is a shared responsibility. For example, in a multi-occupied building, while the landlord might be responsible for general fire safety in communal areas, individual tenants or business owners have responsibility for the areas they control. Effective communication and coordination among all responsible persons are crucial for overall fire safety in such buildings.

Enforcement and Accountability

Local fire and rescue authorities are responsible for enforcing fire safety legislation. The responsible person(s) can face significant penalties, including fines and imprisonment, for non-compliance with fire safety obligations.

The concept of the 'responsible person' is central to fire safety in the UK, emphasising the accountability of those who have control over premises. Understanding and fulfilling these responsibilities are crucial not only for legal compliance but, more importantly, for the safety and wellbeing of everyone using the premises.

Chapter 8:

Responsibilities of the Duty Holder

In the context of UK fire safety regulations, particularly under the Regulatory Reform (Fire Safety) Order 2005, the "duty holder" (often referred to as the "responsible person") is tasked with a range of responsibilities to ensure the safety of people in relation to fire risks in the premises they control. Here's a detailed breakdown of these responsibilities:

1. Conducting Fire Risk Assessments

1. Identifying Hazards: The duty holder must identify potential fire hazards, including sources of ignition, fuel, and oxygen.

2. Evaluating Risks to People: Assessing who may be at risk, especially vulnerable individuals like the elderly, children, or those with disabilities.

3. Regular Review: The risk assessment should be reviewed regularly and updated whenever there are significant changes to the premises or the nature of activities conducted there.

2. Implementing Preventive and Protective Measures

1. Fire Detection and Alarm Systems: Ensuring proper installation and maintenance of fire detection and alarm systems.

2. Firefighting Equipment: Providing appropriate firefighting equipment like extinguishers and ensuring they are easily accessible and maintained.

3. Safety Features and Equipment: Maintaining other fire safety features like fire doors, emergency lighting, and fire-resistant materials.

3. Ensuring Safe Escape Routes

1. Clear Escape Routes: Maintaining clear and safe escape routes at all times.

2. Emergency Exits: Ensuring emergency exits are suitable, clearly marked, and unobstructed.

3. Evacuation Plans: Developing and clearly communicating evacuation plans, including special arrangements for vulnerable individuals.

4. Training and Information

1. Employee Training: Providing regular fire safety training to employees, including instruction on what to do in case of fire.

2. Information to Employees and Occupants: Disseminating information about the risks present in the premises and the fire safety measures in place.

3. Fire Drills and Practice: Conducting regular fire drills to ensure everyone is familiar with evacuation procedures.

5. Record Keeping

1. Documentation: Keeping written records of the fire risk assessment and any significant findings, particularly if the organisation employs five or more people.

2. Maintenance Records: Keeping records of the maintenance of fire safety systems and equipment.

6. Coordination in Shared Premises

1. Cooperation with Others: Coordinating fire safety arrangements with other duty holders in shared premises.

2. Sharing Information: Sharing relevant information about fire risks and safety arrangements with other occupants or duty holders.

7. Compliance and Review

1. Legal Compliance: Ensuring compliance with relevant fire safety legislation.

2. Ongoing Review: Continuously reviewing and updating fire safety measures to ensure they remain effective and compliant with current regulations.

The role of the duty holder is comprehensive and involves a proactive approach to managing fire safety. It's not only about compliance with legal obligations but also about a commitment to ensuring the safety and well-being of people who use or occupy the premises. Effective fire safety management requires regular assessment, maintenance, training, and communication to ensure that risks are minimised and safety is maintained at all times.

Chapter 9:

Responsibilities of Employees

In the UK, employees have specific responsibilities regarding fire safety in the workplace, as outlined by various regulations, including the Regulatory Reform (Fire Safety) Order 2005 and the Health and Safety at Work etc. Act 1974. These responsibilities are integral to ensuring a safe working environment for everyone. Here's a breakdown of these key responsibilities:

1. Compliance with Fire Safety Procedures

- Adhering to Procedures: Employees must follow the fire safety procedures established by their employer. This includes evacuation procedures during drills or in the event of an actual fire.

- Using Equipment Correctly: If trained, employees should use fire safety equipment correctly. Misuse of fire safety equipment, like fire extinguishers or alarms, is generally prohibited.

2. Cooperation and Communication

- Cooperating with Employers: Employees are expected to cooperate with their employers in matters of health and safety, which includes fire safety.

- Reporting Hazards: Employees should report any fire hazards or risks they identify to their employer or the designated fire safety officer. This can include obstructed fire exits, faulty fire safety equipment, or accumulation of combustible materials.

3. Participation in Training and Drills

- Attending Training: Employees are required to participate in fire safety training provided by the employer. This training typically covers how to respond in case of fire, how to evacuate safely, and how to use fire safety equipment.

- Engaging in Fire Drills: Participation in regular fire drills is essential. Drills help employees Familiarise themselves with evacuation routes and procedures, ensuring they know what to do in an emergency.

4. General Fire Safety Awareness

- Understanding Risks: Employees should be aware of the fire risks present in their work environment.

- Following Good Housekeeping Practices: Keeping workspaces tidy to reduce fire risks, such as avoiding clutter that could impede evacuation routes or the functionality of fire safety equipment.

5. Personal Responsibility

- Personal Conduct: Employees should avoid actions that could increase the risk of fire, such as smoking in non-designated areas or misusing electrical equipment.

- Reporting Absences: In some settings, employees may need to report absences from their usual location so that they are not mistakenly searched for during an evacuation.

While the primary responsibility for fire safety in the workplace lies with the employer or the designated 'responsible person,' employees play a crucial role in supporting these efforts. Their responsibilities mainly revolve around compliance, cooperation, communication, participation in safety activities, and general fire safety awareness. A collective approach to fire safety, where both employers and employees are actively engaged, is essential for maintaining a safe working environment.

Chapter 10:

Collaborative Efforts in Ensuring

Fire Safety

Collaborative efforts are crucial in ensuring fire safety in various environments, including workplaces, residential buildings, and public spaces. Effective fire safety management is not just the responsibility of the designated 'responsible person' or duty holder; it requires active participation and cooperation from everyone involved. Here's how collaborative efforts play a vital role in fire safety:

In the Workplace

- Employer and Employee Collaboration: Employers are responsible for implementing fire safety measures, but employees must follow these procedures and contribute to maintaining a safe environment. This includes participating in fire drills, reporting hazards, and adhering to safety guidelines.

- Safety Committees: Many workplaces have safety committees that include representatives from both management and the workforce. These committees can discuss fire safety issues, suggest improvements, and help disseminate fire safety information throughout the organisation.

- Training and Education: Collaborative efforts in training can enhance fire safety awareness. Regular training sessions, workshops, and educational programs keep everyone updated on best practices and evacuation procedures.

In Residential Buildings

- Residents and Management Collaboration: In multi-occupancy buildings, effective fire safety requires cooperation between residents and property management. Residents should follow safety guidelines, report potential hazards, and participate in evacuation drills, if conducted.

- Fire Safety Meetings: Regular meetings or information sessions can be held to discuss fire safety issues, gather feedback from residents, and update everyone on any changes in safety procedures or legislation.

Between Different Organisations

- Inter-Organisational Cooperation: In shared buildings or business complexes, different organisations need to collaborate on fire safety. This might involve coordinating evacuation plans, sharing safety resources, and joint training exercises.

- Public and Private Partnerships: Collaborations between public fire and rescue services and private entities can enhance fire safety. This can include joint fire drills, shared training programs, and community fire safety initiatives.

Involvement of Fire Services

- Consultations and Inspections: Regular consultations with local fire and rescue services can provide valuable insights into improving fire safety measures. Fire services often conduct inspections and can offer expert advice.

- Community Fire Safety Programs: Fire services often run community programs aimed at raising fire safety awareness among the public. Participation in these programs can significantly enhance community-wide fire safety.

Technological Collaboration

- Use of Technology for Fire Safety: Modern technology like fire detection and alarm systems, emergency lighting, and smoke control systems play a crucial role in fire safety. Collaboration between technology providers, installers, and users is vital to ensure these systems are effectively implemented and maintained.

Ensuring fire safety is a multifaceted endeavour that benefits greatly from collaborative efforts. It involves not just compliance with regulations but active engagement and cooperation among all stakeholders. Whether it's in the workplace, residential settings, or wider community, a collaborative approach to fire safety helps to create environments that are safer for everyone.

Chapter 11:

Understanding Risk Assessment

Understanding risk assessment, especially in the context of fire safety and general workplace safety, is crucial for preventing accidents, injuries, and loss of life. A risk assessment is a systematic process of evaluating the potential risks that may be involved in a projected activity or undertaking. Here's a detailed look at understanding risk assessment:

Key Components of Risk Assessment

- Identifying Hazards: This is the first step in a risk assessment. A hazard is anything that has the potential to cause harm. In fire safety, this includes sources of ignition, flammable materials, and the building's layout.

- Deciding Who Might Be Harmed and How: Assess who might be at risk and how they might be harmed. This includes employees, visitors, and in the case of fire risk assessment, potentially adjacent buildings or the public.

- Evaluating Risks: Assess the likelihood and severity of the harm occurring. This involves considering existing safety measures and determining if they are adequate.

- Recording and Implementing Findings: Document the hazards, their associated risks, and the measures to mitigate these risks. Then, implement these measures.

- Reviewing and Updating: Regularly review the risk assessment to ensure it remains relevant, especially if there are significant changes in the working environment or process.

Types of Risk Assessments

- General Risk Assessments: These are conducted in workplaces to identify a range of hazards, from slip and trip hazards to the risks from using machinery or harmful substances.

- Fire Risk Assessments: Specifically focused on identifying fire hazards, evaluating the risks of fire, and implementing measures to prevent fire and ensure safe evacuation in the event of a fire.

- Specialised Risk Assessments: These may be required for specific activities or processes, such as working at heights, using hazardous chemicals, or conducting complex industrial processes.

Principles of Effective Risk Assessment

1. Systematic Approach: Follow a structured process to ensure all potential hazards are identified and assessed.

2. Involvement of Employees: Engaging with employees can provide valuable insights, as they are often most familiar with the potential hazards in their work environment.

3. Proportionality: The level of detail in a risk assessment should be proportionate to the risks. More significant risks require more detailed assessments.

4. Dynamic Process: Risk assessment is not a one-time activity. It should be an ongoing process, adapting and changing as necessary.

5. Preventive Focus: The goal is to identify and mitigate risks before they result in harm.

Legal and Regulatory Framework

In many jurisdictions, conducting risk assessments is not just good practice but a legal requirement. For instance, in the UK, employers are required under the Health and Safety at Work etc.

Act 1974 and the Management of Health and Safety at Work Regulations 1999 to carry out risk assessments.

Understanding risk assessment is about recognising potential hazards, evaluating the risks associated with these hazards, and implementing appropriate measures to mitigate them. It is a critical part of managing health and safety in any environment, from workplaces to public spaces. Effective risk assessments help to prevent accidents and injuries, creating a safer environment for everyone.

Chapter 12:

What is a Fire Risk Assessment?

A Fire Risk Assessment is a systematic evaluation conducted to identify the potential fire hazards, assess the risk of fire, and determine measures to minimise or eliminate the risk of fire in a particular setting, such as a building or workplace. This process is crucial for ensuring fire safety and is a legal requirement in many jurisdictions, including the UK. Here's an overview of what a Fire Risk Assessment entails:

Key Elements of a Fire Risk Assessment

1. Identifying Fire Hazards: This includes finding potential sources of ignition (like heaters or electrical equipment), fuel (such as paper, chemicals, or textiles), and oxygen sources (like air conditioning or medical oxygen supplies).

2. Identifying People at Risk: Determining who may be at risk in the event of a fire, especially focusing on vulnerable individuals like the elderly, children, or those with disabilities.

3. Evaluating, Removing, or Reducing the Risks: Assessing the likelihood of a fire starting and the potential consequences if it does. This involves evaluating existing fire safety measures (like fire detection systems, alarms, and extinguishers) and determining whether additional measures are needed.

4. Recording Findings, Preparing an Emergency Plan, and Providing Training: Documenting the significant findings of the assessment, preparing an emergency plan tailored to the premises, and providing adequate training for staff or occupants.

5. Reviewing and Updating the Assessment Regularly: Fire risk assessments should be reviewed regularly, particularly when there are changes to the building, occupancy, or the type of activities taking place.

Purpose of a Fire Risk Assessment

1. Prevention of Fire: The primary goal is to prevent fires from occurring.

2. Safety of Occupants: Ensuring the safety of people in the building by providing effective means of escape.

3. Compliance with Legislation: In many regions, including the UK, conducting a fire risk assessment is a legal requirement for most types of buildings, especially workplaces and public access buildings.

Legal Context in the UK

Under the Regulatory Reform (Fire Safety) Order 2005 in England and Wales, the Fire (Scotland) Act 2005, and the Fire and Rescue Services (Northern Ireland) Order 2006, the 'responsible person' (usually the employer, building owner, or occupier) must conduct a fire risk assessment.

Conducting a Fire Risk Assessment

1. Professional Assessment or DIY: While smaller businesses or premises can often conduct the assessment themselves, larger or more complex buildings may require a professional fire risk assessor.

2. Involving Employees and Occupants: It's important to involve employees or residents in the process, as they can provide valuable insights into potential hazards and risks.

A Fire Risk Assessment is a fundamental aspect of fire safety management. It's not just about compliance with legal obligations but is also a proactive measure to ensure the safety and well-being of people in various settings. Regular review and adaptation of the fire risk assessment are essential to maintain an effective fire safety strategy.

The Importance of Fire Risk Assessments

Fire risk assessments are crucial for several reasons, particularly in the context of ensuring safety in workplaces, public buildings, and residential properties. Their importance can be understood from multiple perspectives:

1. Safety and Prevention

1. Preventing Fires: By identifying potential fire hazards, a fire risk assessment helps in implementing measures to prevent fires from occurring.

2. Saving Lives: A key aspect of fire risk assessments is to ensure there are adequate means of escape, which directly contributes to saving lives in the event of a fire.

3. Protecting Property: Fire risk assessments help in protecting properties from the devastating effects of fires, thereby safeguarding investments.

2. Legal Compliance

1. Adherence to Regulations: In many jurisdictions, conducting a fire risk assessment is a legal requirement. For example, in the UK, it's mandated under the Regulatory Reform (Fire Safety) Order 2005.

2. Avoiding Penalties: Failure to carry out an adequate fire risk assessment can result in legal action, fines, and in severe cases, imprisonment for responsible individuals.

3. Financial Implications

1. Reducing Insurance Premiums: Often, a comprehensive fire risk assessment can lead to reduced insurance premiums, as it demonstrates a commitment to maintaining safety standards.

2. Cost Savings: By preventing fires, organisations can avoid the significant costs associated with fire damage, including repairs, replacements, and potential business interruptions.

4. Ethical and Moral Responsibility

1. Duty of Care: Employers and building owners have a moral and ethical duty to ensure the safety of their employees, residents, or visitors.

2. Community Trust: Conducting regular and thorough fire risk assessments builds trust among employees, customers, and the community, demonstrating a commitment to safety and well-being.

5. Risk Management

1. Proactive Approach: Fire risk assessments allow for a proactive approach to risk management, identifying risks before they result in incidents.

2. Informed Decision Making: They provide essential information that helps in making informed decisions about fire safety measures and emergency preparedness.

6. Emergency Preparedness

- Planning for Emergencies: Fire risk assessments are integral to emergency planning, ensuring that effective evacuation plans are in place and that people are trained to respond appropriately in case of a fire.

7. Continuity and Reputation

- Business Continuity: By preventing fires, organisations can ensure the continuity of their operations.

- Maintaining Reputation: Effective fire risk management helps in maintaining an organisation's reputation for safety and responsibility.

The importance of fire risk assessments lies not only in fulfilling legal obligations but also in the broader context of ensuring safety, preventing property damage, managing risks, and upholding ethical standards. Regularly conducted and updated fire risk assessments are fundamental to creating a safe and secure environment for all occupants and visitors of a building.

How Often Should a Fire Risk Assessment Be Carried Out?

The frequency of conducting a fire risk assessment can vary depending on several factors, such as the type of premises, the nature of the activities conducted there, and any changes to the building or its use. However, there are general guidelines to consider:

General Guidelines

- Regular Reviews: Even if there are no significant changes, it's recommended to review the fire risk assessment regularly. A common practice is to conduct a formal review annually.

- After Significant Changes: Whenever there are significant changes to the premises, such as renovations, extensions, changes in building use, or the introduction of new equipment or processes, the fire risk assessment should be updated.

- Following a Fire Incident: If a fire occurs, it's crucial to review and update the fire risk assessment to incorporate what was learned from the incident and to prevent future occurrences.

- Changes in Legislation: If there are changes in fire safety legislation or regulations, reassessments may be necessary to ensure continued compliance.

Specific Circumstances

- High-Risk Environments: In premises with higher fire risks, such as industrial sites, kitchens, or areas where flammable materials are stored, more frequent assessments might be necessary.

- Public Access Buildings: Places like schools, hospitals, and shopping centres, which have high public footfall, may require more frequent reviews due to the complexity and changing nature of fire risks.

- Multiple Occupancy Buildings: In buildings with multiple businesses or tenants, changes by one occupant can affect the overall fire safety of the building, necessitating more regular assessments.

Legal Requirements

- In the UK, under the Regulatory Reform (Fire Safety) Order 2005, there is no specified interval for fire risk assessments. However, it is the duty holder's responsibility to ensure that the assessment is 'suitable and sufficient' and remains up to date.

Best Practices

- Documentation: Always document the date of the fire risk assessment and any subsequent reviews or updates.

- Professional Advice: If unsure about the frequency, it's advisable to seek professional advice from fire safety experts.

While there is no one-size-fits-all answer to how often a fire risk assessment should be carried out, the key is to ensure it remains current and reflective of any changes in the premises or activities conducted there. Regular reviews, vigilance to changes, and responsiveness to incidents are crucial in maintaining effective fire safety management.

Chapter 13:

Conducting a Fire Risk Assessment

Conducting a fire risk assessment is a systematic process essential for identifying fire hazards, evaluating the risk of fire, and determining measures to mitigate or eliminate these risks. Here's a step-by-step guide on how to conduct a fire risk assessment:

1. Identify Fire Hazards

- Sources of Ignition: Look for potential sources of ignition, such as electrical equipment, heating appliances, open flames, or smoking areas.

- Sources of Fuel: Identify materials that could fuel a fire, like paper, wood, plastics, chemicals, or flammable liquids.

- Sources of Oxygen: Consider sources of oxygen that could intensify a fire, including air conditioning systems or medical oxygen supplies.

2. Identify People at Risk

- Occupants of the Premises: Consider who uses the premises, including employees, visitors, and customers.

- Vulnerable Individuals: Pay special attention to people who might be particularly at risk, such as the elderly, children, or those with disabilities.

- External Individuals: Consider the risk to neighbouring properties or the general public.

3. Evaluate the Risk and Implement Controls

- Evaluate the Likelihood and Impact: Assess how likely it is that a fire could start and what the consequences could be.

- Implement Preventative Measures: Based on the evaluation, implement measures to either remove or reduce the fire hazards. This could include replacing flammable materials with less flammable ones, ensuring electrical equipment is maintained, or enforcing a no-smoking policy.

- Fire Detection and Warning Systems: Ensure adequate fire detection systems (like smoke alarms) are in place and functioning.

- Emergency Exits and Routes: Make sure there are enough safe emergency exits, and that escape routes are clearly marked and unobstructed.

- Firefighting Equipment: Provide appropriate firefighting equipment (such as fire extinguishers) and ensure it's easily accessible.

4. Record, Plan, and Train

1. Record Your Findings: Document the hazards identified, the people at risk, and the measures put in place to mitigate these risks.

2. Develop an Emergency Plan: Prepare a clear plan for what to do in case of a fire, including evacuation procedures.

3. Training and Information: Ensure that staff and relevant individuals are trained on fire safety, know how to evacuate, and understand the fire risks.

5. Review and Update the Assessment

1. Regular Reviews: Fire risk assessments should be reviewed regularly and updated whenever there are significant changes to the premises, the nature of the work conducted, or the people present.

2. After an Incident: If a fire or near-miss occurs, review the assessment in light of this incident.

Best Practices

- Professional Assistance: For complex environments or large premises, consider hiring a professional fire safety consultant to conduct the assessment.

- Involvement of Employees: Engage employees in the process, as they can provide valuable insights into potential hazards and risks.

- Compliance with Legislation: Ensure that the assessment and subsequent actions comply with local fire safety legislation and standards.

A fire risk assessment is a critical component of fire safety management. It's not just a one-time activity but an ongoing process that should be integral to the regular operations of any premises. By systematically identifying hazards, evaluating risks, implementing controls, and continuously reviewing and updating the assessment, you can significantly reduce the risk of fire and ensure the safety of everyone involved.

Identifying Fire Hazards

Identifying fire hazards is a fundamental part of a fire risk assessment and is essential for ensuring fire safety in any environment, whether it's a workplace, residential building, or public space. Fire hazards are conditions or activities that increase the probability of a fire occurring or can exacerbate the severity of a fire. Here's a guide to identifying fire hazards:

1. Sources of Ignition

- Electrical Equipment: Faulty or overloaded electrical equipment, such as frayed cords, overloaded power outlets, or malfunctioning appliances.

- Heating Appliances: Heaters, boilers, and furnaces, especially if they are close to combustible materials.

- Smoking Areas: Improper disposal of cigarettes or smoking in non-designated areas.

- Open Flames: Candles, lanterns, or any open flames used either for decoration or in work processes.

- Hot Work: Activities like welding, cutting, or grinding that produce sparks or flames.

- Arson: Intentional setting of fires, a risk that may be mitigated by securing premises against unauthorised entry.

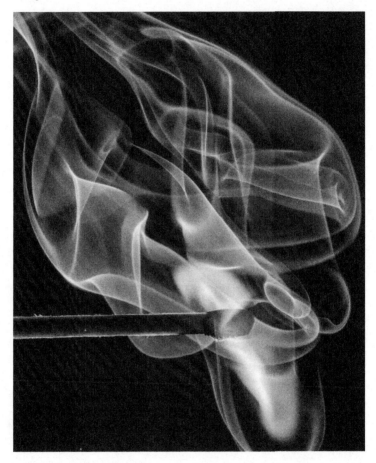

2. Sources of Fuel

- Combustible Materials: Paper, wood, plastics, textiles, and rubbish that can easily catch fire.

- Flammable Liquids and Gases: Fuels, solvents, paints, varnishes, and aerosols.

- Accumulations of Dust: In certain settings, dust from wood, flour, sugar, or other materials can be highly combustible.

- Overstocked Inventory: Excessive storage of products, especially if combustible, can increase fire load.

3. Sources of Oxygen

- Ventilation Systems: Can supply a steady stream of air that may feed a fire.

- Oxygen Cylinders: Medical or industrial oxygen can intensify a fire.

- Natural Air Flow: Open windows, doors, or other openings can provide oxygen to fuel a fire.

4. Human Factors

- Negligence or Lack of Awareness: Unattended equipment, misuse of appliances, or not following safety procedures.

- Poor Housekeeping: Cluttered workspaces can contribute to fires and hinder escape routes.

- Improper Storage: Storing chemicals or flammable materials improperly.

5. Environmental Factors

- Building Layout and Design: Certain designs may facilitate the spread of fire.

- Electrical Wiring and Gas Lines: Old or poorly maintained wiring and gas lines can be significant hazards.

Conducting the Identification Process

- Walkthrough Inspections: Regularly walk through the premises to identify potential hazards.

- Consultation with Employees and Residents: Often, those who use the space daily are best placed to identify hazards.

- Professional Fire Safety Audits: For complex environments, a professional audit can help identify hazards that may be overlooked.

Identifying fire hazards is an ongoing process and should be part of a regular safety routine. Once hazards are identified, appropriate measures can be taken to eliminate or reduce the risk of fire. This proactive approach is key to maintaining a safe environment for everyone.

Evaluating the Risk and Identifying Control Measures

Evaluating the risk and identifying control measures are crucial steps in the fire risk assessment process. Once potential fire hazards have been identified, the next step is to evaluate how likely these hazards are to cause a fire, assess the potential severity of such a fire, and then determine appropriate measures to control or mitigate these risks. Here's an overview of this process:

Evaluating the Risk

- Likelihood of a Fire Occurring: Assess how likely each identified hazard is to cause a fire. This includes considering factors like the condition of electrical equipment, the frequency of hot work activities, or the presence of ignition sources near combustible materials.

- Potential Severity: Evaluate the potential severity if a fire were to occur. Consider the type and amount of combustible materials present, the building layout, and the presence of vulnerable individuals.

- Existing Control Measures: Review current fire safety measures in place, such as fire detection and alarm systems, fire extinguishers, and emergency escape routes. Assess their adequacy and effectiveness.

- Risk Rating: Often, risks are rated based on their severity and likelihood, such as 'high', 'medium', or 'low'. This helps prioritise the risks that need more immediate attention.

Identifying Control Measures

Once the risks have been evaluated, the next step is to identify measures that can control or reduce these risks. This involves a combination of removing hazards where possible and reducing the likelihood or impact of a fire if one were to occur.

- Removing or Reducing Hazards: This might involve replacing flammable materials with less flammable alternatives, ensuring good housekeeping to minimise combustible waste, or improving the maintenance of electrical equipment.

- Fire Detection and Warning Systems: Ensure that appropriate fire detection systems are in place and regularly maintained. This might include smoke detectors, heat detectors, or manual call points.

- Firefighting Equipment: Provide suitable firefighting equipment like fire extinguishers, and ensure staff are trained in their use.

- Emergency Escape Routes: Ensure that emergency escape routes are clearly marked, unobstructed, and known to all occupants. Practice evacuation drills regularly.

- Training and Information: Regular training and information sessions for staff and occupants on fire safety procedures and the correct action to take in the event of a fire.

- Special Measures for Vulnerable Individuals: Implement additional measures for individuals who may need assistance during an evacuation, such as those with mobility impairments.

- Reviewing and Updating Risk Assessments: The identified control measures should be reviewed and updated regularly, especially if there are changes in the use of the premises, the building layout, or the nature of work activities.

Documenting the Process

- Record Keeping: Keep detailed records of the risk evaluation and the control measures identified. This documentation should be accessible and updated as necessary.

Evaluating the risk and identifying control measures are integral to a proactive fire safety strategy. This approach not only helps in preventing fires but also ensures that, in the event of a fire, its impact is minimised, and people can safely evacuate. Regular review and adaptation of these measures are key to maintaining effective fire safety management.

Chapter 14:

Recording, Planning,

Implementing, and Reviewing

Recording, planning, implementing, and reviewing are essential steps in the fire risk assessment process and in maintaining effective fire safety management. Each of these steps plays a critical role in ensuring that fire risks are properly managed and that safety measures are up to date and effective.

1. Recording

- Documenting Findings: All significant findings from the fire risk assessment should be recorded. This includes the hazards identified, the evaluation of the risks, and the measures put in place to control those risks.

- Legal Requirement: In many jurisdictions, there is a legal requirement to record the findings of a fire risk assessment, especially if the organisation has a certain number of employees (e.g., five or more in the UK).

- Accessibility: The records should be accessible and understandable to all relevant parties, including employees, safety representatives, and fire safety officers.

2. Planning

- Developing an Action Plan: Based on the risk assessment, develop a plan to implement the necessary fire safety measures. This plan should prioritise actions based on the level of risk.

- Allocating Resources: Ensure that sufficient resources (time, budget, personnel) are allocated to implement the fire safety measures.

- Emergency Plans: Develop clear and concise emergency plans, including evacuation procedures, roles and responsibilities during an emergency, and contact information for emergency services.

3. Implementing

- Putting Measures into Action: Implement the control measures as planned. This may involve physical changes to the premises, purchasing fire safety equipment, or organising training sessions.

- Communication and Training: Inform all relevant parties about the fire safety measures in place. Conduct regular fire safety training and drills to ensure everyone knows what to do in case of a fire.

- Continual Improvement: Fire safety should be seen as an ongoing process, with continual monitoring and improvement of practices and procedures.

4. Reviewing

- Regular Reviews: Fire risk assessments and safety measures should be reviewed regularly. This ensures that any changes in the premises, processes, or the number of people on site are taken into account.

- After an Incident: If a fire or a near-miss occurs, review the risk assessment and safety measures in light of this incident to understand what happened and why, and to prevent recurrence.

- Changes in Legislation: Stay updated with any changes in fire safety legislation or best practices and review your procedures to ensure compliance.

Recording, planning, implementing, and reviewing are interconnected stages that ensure a comprehensive approach to fire safety management. Effective management is not a one-time event but a continuous cycle of assessment, action, and revaluation. This cycle helps to create a safe environment, prevent fires, and ensure a prepared and informed response in the event of a fire.

Fire Risk Assessment Tools

Fire risk assessment tools are instrumental in helping businesses, organisations, and individuals effectively identify and manage fire risks. These tools can range from simple checklists to sophisticated software programs, each designed to facilitate the process of conducting a thorough fire risk assessment. Here's an overview of various types of fire risk assessment tools:

1. Checklists and Templates

1. Basic Checklists: Simple checklists cover fundamental fire safety points, including identifying fire hazards (like sources of ignition and fuel), evaluating escape routes, and ensuring the availability of firefighting equipment.

2. Templates: More detailed templates guide users through each step of a fire risk assessment, often including sections for recording findings, evaluating risks, and noting action items.

2. Software and Applications

1. Dedicated Fire Risk Assessment Software: These specialised programs offer a comprehensive approach, guiding users through the entire assessment process, and often include features for scheduling reviews, managing documentation, and tracking compliance.

2. Mobile Apps: Mobile applications provide the convenience of conducting assessments directly on-site, with features for capturing photos, setting reminders, and sharing reports.

3. Guideline Documents and Handbooks

- Fire Safety Handbooks: Detailed handbooks provide in-depth guidance on how to conduct fire risk assessments, often tailored to specific types of premises like offices, schools, or industrial facilities.

- Regulatory Guidelines: Guidelines issued by fire safety authorities or government bodies outline the legal requirements and best practices in fire risk assessment.

4. Online Resources and Platforms

- Interactive Websites: Some websites offer interactive tools, including step-by-step guides, FAQs, and resources tailored to specific sectors or building types.

- Educational Videos and Webinars: Online video resources can be valuable for understanding the principles of fire risk assessment and seeing real-world examples of how to identify and mitigate risks.

5. Professional Consultation Tools

- Risk Assessment Matrix: Used by professionals, these matrices help in evaluating the likelihood and impact of fire risks, aiding in prioritising risk mitigation efforts.

- Site Survey Tools: Tools for conducting detailed site surveys, including thermal imaging cameras and gas detection equipment, used to identify hidden hazards.

6. Customised Tools for Specialised Environments

- Industry-Specific Tools: Certain industries may have customised tools that address the unique fire hazards associated with their specific processes or environments, like chemical plants or healthcare facilities.

Choosing the right fire risk assessment depends on various factors, including the size and complexity of the premises, the nature of the activities conducted, and the resources available. While smaller businesses might find checklists and basic software adequate, larger organisations or those in high-risk industries might benefit from more sophisticated software or professional consultations such as that are provided by Acorn Safety Services. Regardless of the tool used, the key is to ensure that the fire risk assessment is thorough, up-to-date, and compliant with relevant fire safety regulations.

Case Study: Using Fire Risk Assessment Tools Effectively

This case study examines the successful implementation of fire risk assessment by a mid-sized manufacturing company in the UK. With a workforce of 200 employees that operates in a facility which includes manufacturing areas, storage units, and office spaces. The company recognised the need to enhance its fire safety practices and chose to integrate advanced fire risk assessments to ensure compliance with the Regulatory Reform (Fire Safety) Order 2005.

Background

- Their facility had complex fire safety requirements due to the nature of its manufacturing processes, which involved the use of flammable materials. Prior to the implementation, the company relied on basic checklists and manual inspections, which were found to be inadequate during an audit by Acorn Safety Services.

Implementation

- Selection of Tools: They selected a comprehensive fire risk assessment for industrial settings. The assessment included hazard identification, risk evaluation, compliance tracking, and reporting.

- Training: Key staff members, including safety officers and facility managers, were trained in line with the assessment. This training included understanding how to interpret results and follow up on recommended actions.

- Integration: The assessment and subsequent processes were incorporated into the company's daily operations. Regular inspections were then conducted, with data being instantly uploaded to the central system.

Key Actions and Results

- Identifying Hazards: Acorn helped in systematically identifying potential fire hazards in different areas of the facility, such as improper storage of flammable materials and overloaded electrical outlets.

- Risk Evaluation and Compliance: Acorn's fire consultant allowed for a more nuanced risk evaluation, taking into account the likelihood and potential impact of identified hazards. It also ensured that all fire safety measures were compliant with current regulations.

- Preventive Measures: Based on the software's recommendations, the business implemented several preventive measures, including upgrading fire detection systems, improving housekeeping practices to reduce combustible waste, and revising emergency evacuation plans.

- Training and Drills: There were scheduled regular fire safety training for employees and organised evacuation drills, enhancing overall fire safety awareness.

- Maintenance and Review: A schedule facilitated regular maintenance checks of fire safety equipment and reviews of the fire risk assessment.

Outcome

- Enhanced Safety: There was a marked improvement in overall fire safety within the facility, with a significant reduction in fire-related incidents.

- Compliance: The business reported full compliance with fire safety regulations during a subsequent external audit.

- Employee Confidence: The implementation of a robust fire risk assessment increased confidence among employees regarding their safety at work.

Conclusion

- The businesses experience highlights the effectiveness of integrating specialised fire risk assessments in managing complex fire safety needs. The proactive approach not only ensured regulatory compliance but also fostered a safer work environment. This case underscores the importance of utilising appropriate companies in fire risk management and demonstrates the benefits of investing in advanced safety solutions.

Chapter 15:

Risk Reduction Strategies

Risk reduction strategies in fire safety involve a comprehensive approach that includes preventive measures, mitigative measures, and emergency planning. These strategies aim to reduce the likelihood of a fire occurring, limit the impact if a fire does occur, and ensure preparedness for an effective response during an emergency. Here's an overview of each component:

1. Preventive Measures

Preventive measures are actions taken to prevent a fire from starting in the first place. They are critical in minimising the risk of fire and can include:

- Regular Maintenance: Ensuring electrical systems, heating equipment, and other potential sources of ignition are well-maintained and in good working order.

- Safe Storage Practices: Properly storing flammable and combustible materials away from ignition sources.

- Good Housekeeping: Keeping workplaces and premises clean and free of unnecessary combustible materials that could fuel a fire.

- Fire Safety Training: Providing regular training for employees and residents on fire safety practices, including how to prevent fires.

- Implementing No Smoking Policies: Designating specific smoking areas and enforcing strict no-smoking policies in hazardous areas.

- Control of Heat Sources: Managing and monitoring heat sources, such as industrial processes or cooking areas, to prevent overheating and ignition.

2. Mitigative Measures

Mitigative measures are designed to reduce the severity and impact of a fire if one does occur. These measures include:

- Installation of Fire Detection and Suppression Systems: Implementing systems like smoke alarms, fire sprinklers, and fire extinguishers to detect and suppress fires quickly.

- Fire-Resistant Materials and Construction: Using fire-resistant building materials and incorporating fire-resistant design elements to slow the spread of fire.

- Compartmentation: Dividing premises into compartments to contain fires and prevent their spread.

- Ensuring Adequate Firefighting Access: Providing clear access routes for firefighting personnel and equipment.

- Regular Inspections and Testing: Regularly inspecting and testing fire safety systems to ensure they are functioning correctly.

3. Emergency Planning

Emergency planning involves preparing for a fire incident to ensure a coordinated and effective response. Key aspects include:

- Evacuation Plans: Developing clear evacuation procedures and ensuring all occupants are familiar with them.

- Training and Drills: Conducting regular fire drills to practice evacuation procedures and prepare occupants for a real emergency.

- Emergency Roles and Responsibilities: Assigning specific roles and responsibilities to staff members during an emergency, such as fire wardens or first aiders.

- Communication Plans: Establishing effective communication strategies to alert occupants in the event of a fire and to communicate with emergency services.

- Emergency Lighting and Signage: Installing and maintaining emergency lighting and clear signage to facilitate evacuation.

Risk reduction strategies in fire safety encompass a broad range of measures, from preventing fires to preparing for an effective response when they occur. By combining preventive and mitigative measures with thorough emergency planning, organisations and individuals can significantly reduce the risk associated with fire, protect property, and most importantly, save lives.

Chapter 16:

Creating an Emergency Evacuation

Plan

Creating an emergency evacuation plan is a critical component of fire safety and emergency preparedness. It involves developing a clear, effective strategy for evacuating all occupants safely and quickly from a building or area in case of a fire or other emergencies. Here's a guide on how to create an emergency evacuation plan:

1. Understand the Layout of the Building

- Floor Plans: Familiarise yourself with the building's layout, including all possible exits, stairwells, corridors, and emergency escape routes.

- Identify Exits: Clearly mark all emergency exits and ensure they are easily accessible and free from obstructions.

2. Identify and Assess Risks

1. Risk Assessment: Conduct a thorough risk assessment to identify potential hazards and high-risk areas within the building.

2. Special Needs: Consider the needs of all building occupants, including children, the elderly, and individuals with disabilities who may require additional assistance.

3. Designate Primary and Secondary Escape Routes

1. Multiple Routes: Establish primary and secondary escape routes from all areas of the building. This ensures alternatives if the primary route is blocked or unsafe.

2. Clear Signage: Install clear, visible signs along escape routes and at exits.

4. Assign Roles and Responsibilities

- Fire Wardens: Designate fire wardens or marshals who will oversee the evacuation process, assist with headcounts, and help those who need assistance.

- Communication Leads: Assign individuals responsible for communicating with emergency services and disseminating information to occupants.

5. Develop an Evacuation Procedure

- Clear Instructions: Outline specific steps for evacuation, including how to safely exit the building, where to go once outside, and how to report to a designated safe assembly area.

- Special Procedures for High-Risk Areas: Develop specific procedures for areas with higher risks, like kitchens, laboratories, or areas with hazardous materials.

6. Establish a Safe Assembly Area

- Safe Location: Choose an assembly area at a safe distance from the building where occupants can gather after evacuation.

- Headcounts: Ensure that procedures are in place for taking headcounts or roll calls to verify that all occupants have safely evacuated.

7. Communicate and Train

- Inform Occupants: Make sure all building occupants are aware of the evacuation plan. Distribute maps and instructions as necessary.

- Regular Drills: Conduct regular evacuation drills to ensure everyone knows what to do and where to go in an emergency.

8. Review and Update the Plan Regularly

- Continuous Improvement: Regularly review and update the evacuation plan, especially after drills, changes in building layout, occupancy, or after an actual emergency.

- Feedback and Learning: Incorporate feedback from drills and emergencies to improve the plan.

9. Coordinate with Local Emergency Services

- Professional Input: If possible, involve local fire and emergency services in the planning process for expert advice and recommendations.

- Emergency Access: Ensure that emergency services have easy access to the building and are aware of key features of your evacuation plan.

An effective emergency evacuation plan is essential for ensuring the safety of all occupants in the event of a fire or other emergencies. It requires careful planning, clear communication, and regular practice to be effective. By being prepared and regularly reviewing and practicing the plan, you can significantly improve the safety and well-being of everyone in the building.

Staff Training and Responsibilities in an Emergency

Staff training and clearly defined responsibilities are crucial components of an organisation's emergency preparedness and response plan. In the context of fire safety or other emergencies, ensuring that staff are well-trained and aware of their roles can significantly impact the effectiveness of the response and the safety of all involved. Here's an overview of staff training and responsibilities in an emergency:

Staff Training

- Emergency Procedures: Regular training on emergency procedures, including evacuation routes, assembly points, and the use of fire safety equipment like extinguishers and fire alarms.

- Fire Safety Education: Educating staff on fire prevention practices, identifying fire hazards, and understanding the nature of fire and smoke.

- First Aid and CPR: Providing training in first aid, CPR, and the use of automated external defibrillators (AEDs), especially for designated first aiders.

- Specialised Training: For staff in roles with specific safety responsibilities, like fire wardens or safety officers, specialised training is necessary to carry out their roles effectively.

- Drills and Simulations: Conducting regular fire drills and emergency simulations to ensure staff are familiar with procedures and can respond appropriately under pressure.

Staff Responsibilities in an Emergency

- Fire Wardens/Marshals: Responsible for overseeing the evacuation of a designated area, ensuring that everyone leaves safely, checking restrooms and closed spaces, and helping those who need assistance.

- First Aiders: Providing immediate medical assistance where necessary, managing first aid supplies, and assisting vulnerable individuals.

- Communication Roles: Maintaining communication with emergency services, coordinating with management, and disseminating information to staff and occupants.

- Shut-Down Procedures: Certain staff may be responsible for shutting down critical equipment or systems safely in an emergency to prevent further hazards.

- Headcount or Roll Call: Ensuring that all staff, visitors, and personnel are accounted for at the assembly point.

General Staff Responsibilities

- Evacuation: Knowing when and how to evacuate safely, including understanding primary and secondary escape routes.

- Reporting Hazards: Reporting potential safety hazards or suspicious activities that could lead to an emergency.

- Staying Informed: Keeping updated with changes in emergency procedures and attending scheduled training sessions.

- Supporting Colleagues: Assisting colleagues, visitors, and others during an evacuation, especially those who may need additional help.

Post-Emergency Responsibilities

- Debriefing: Participating in post-incident debriefings to provide feedback and learn from the event.

- Emotional Support: Providing or seeking emotional support, as emergencies can be traumatic experiences.

Effective staff training and clear delineation of responsibilities are essential for a coordinated and efficient response to emergencies. Regular training, drills, and clear communication ensure that staff members are not only aware of their roles but are also prepared to act swiftly and decisively to safeguard their safety and that of others.

Record Keeping

Record keeping is a fundamental aspect of risk management, especially in the context of fire safety and emergency planning. Maintaining accurate and comprehensive records is crucial for ensuring compliance with legal requirements, facilitating effective risk management, and enhancing overall safety. Here's an overview of what records should be kept and how they can be used for ongoing risk management:

What Records Should Be Kept?

- Fire Risk Assessment Reports: Detailed documentation of each fire risk assessment conducted, including the date, findings, risk evaluations, and recommended control measures.

- Training Records: Records of all training sessions provided to staff, including fire safety training, first aid, emergency response training, and records of participant attendance.

- Maintenance Logs: Documentation of the regular maintenance, testing, and servicing of fire safety equipment such as fire extinguishers, alarm systems, sprinklers, emergency lighting, and any safety-critical elements.

- Incident Reports: Records of any fire-related incidents or near-misses, including details of the event, how it was managed, and any lessons learned.

- Drill Records: Details of all fire and emergency drills conducted, including dates, effectiveness, staff participation, and any areas identified for improvement.

- Evacuation Plans and Procedures: Copies of current evacuation plans and procedures, including any changes or updates made.

- Inspection Certificates: Certificates and reports from external inspections or audits conducted by fire safety consultants or regulatory bodies.

- Employee Feedback: Documentation of any feedback or suggestions from employees regarding fire safety, which can be valuable for identifying potential improvements.

Using Records for Ongoing Risk Management

- Identifying Trends and Patterns: Reviewing records over time can help identify trends or recurring issues, allowing for proactive measures to address them.

- Compliance Monitoring: Keeping thorough records ensures that the organisation can demonstrate compliance with fire safety legislation and standards.

- Informing Risk Assessments: Historical data from records can inform future risk assessments, ensuring they are based on accurate and relevant information.

- Improving Training Programs: Training records can be used to assess the effectiveness of training programs and identify areas where additional training may be needed.

- Enhancing Emergency Preparedness: Analysis of drill records and incident reports can improve emergency plans and procedures, making them more effective.

- Evidence in Case of Incidents: In the event of a fire or other incident, records provide essential evidence for insurance claims, investigations, or legal proceedings.

- Continuous Improvement: Regularly reviewing and updating records contributes to a culture of continuous improvement in fire safety and risk management practices.

Effective record keeping is not just a regulatory requirement but a key component of a comprehensive risk management strategy. It helps in tracking the implementation and effectiveness of safety measures, ensuring compliance, and facilitating continuous improvement in fire safety and emergency preparedness.

Chapter 17:

Engaging Fire Safety Professionals

Engaging fire safety professionals such as Acorn Safety Services is an important consideration for businesses and organisations to ensure comprehensive fire safety management. There are circumstances when seeking external help is necessary, and selecting a competent fire safety advisor is crucial for effective consultation. Here's a guide on when to engage fire safety professionals and how to choose the right advisor:

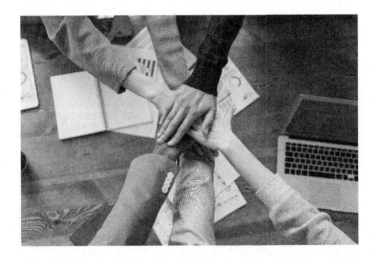

When to Seek External Help

- Complex Premises: For buildings with complex layouts, multiple occupants, or specialised uses (like industrial facilities or healthcare settings), professional advice can be invaluable.

- Lack of In-House Expertise: If an organisation lacks in-house expertise in fire safety, external consultants can provide the necessary specialised knowledge.

- After Significant Changes: Following major renovations, changes in building use, or occupancy, an expert can help reassess fire risks and update safety plans accordingly.

- Compliance with Regulations: To ensure compliance with fire safety regulations, especially if there have been updates or changes in legislation.

- Following an Incident: After a fire or near-miss incident, professionals can help investigate the causes, assess the effectiveness of current measures, and recommend improvements.

- Risk Assessment Review: For a comprehensive review of the existing fire risk assessment, especially if there are concerns about its adequacy or thoroughness.

Selecting a Competent Fire Safety Advisor

1. Qualifications and Certification: Look for advisors with recognised qualifications in fire safety management. Certifications from reputable bodies can be a good indicator of competence.

2. Experience: Consider their experience, especially in dealing with similar types of buildings or organisations. Experience in your specific industry or sector can be particularly beneficial.

3. References and Reviews: Ask for references or check reviews from other clients to gauge their reliability and the quality of their work.

4. Knowledge of Legislation: Ensure they have up-to-date knowledge of current fire safety legislation and best practices.

5. Insurance: Check that they have appropriate professional indemnity insurance, which can provide peace of mind about the advice they provide.

6. Approach and Methodology: Discuss their approach to fire safety to ensure it aligns with your organisation's needs. Understanding their methodology will give insight into how thorough and comprehensive their services are.

7. Communication Skills: A competent advisor should be able to communicate complex information clearly and effectively. Good communication is essential for understanding risks and the measures required to mitigate them.

8. Ongoing Support: Consider whether they offer ongoing support and advice, which can be crucial for maintaining fire safety standards over time.

Engaging a fire safety professional can bring valuable expertise and insights to your fire safety strategy, ensuring that risks are appropriately managed and that your organisation remains compliant with fire safety regulations. The key is to select an advisor who is not only qualified and experienced but also aligns with the specific needs and circumstances of your organisation.

Case Study: Learning from Past Incidents - How Proper Fire Risk Assessment Saved Lives and Property

This case study examines a critical incident at a client's site, a large textile manufacturing plant in the UK, where a proper fire risk assessment played a pivotal role in averting a potentially catastrophic fire, highlighting the importance of compliance with fire safety regulations and the legal implications of non-compliance.

Background

1. The company had a history of minor fire-related incidents, primarily due to the flammable nature of textile materials and the extensive use of electrical machinery. Following a near-miss incident that caused minor injuries and production disruption, the company decided to overhaul its fire safety protocols.

Incident Overview

2. Six months after revamping its fire safety measures, a fire broke out in one of the manufacturing units due to an electrical fault. However, the severity of the incident was significantly mitigated thanks to the recent improvements in their fire risk assessment and safety measures.

How Proper Fire Risk Assessment Saved Lives and Property

3. Early Detection: Enhanced fire detection systems, installed as part of the risk assessment recommendations, quickly identified the fire, allowing for prompt evacuation and response.

4. Effective Evacuation Plan: A well-practiced evacuation plan ensured all employees exited the building safely, preventing injuries.

5. Reduced Fire Spread: Improved storage practices for flammable materials and the introduction of fire-resistant barriers helped contain the fire to a small area.

6. Rapid Emergency Response: The clear communication channels established with local fire services ensured a swift response, minimising property damage.

Legal Implications

- Compliance with Fire Safety Regulations: The company's adherence to the Regulatory Reform (Fire Safety) Order 2005 was instrumental in their effective response to the fire.

- Avoidance of Legal Action: The company's robust fire safety measures and compliance with legal standards protected them from potential legal action, which could have arisen from negligence or non-compliance.

Non-Compliance Penalties

- Avoidance of Fines and Prosecution: By complying with fire safety regulations, they avoided substantial fines and legal repercussions that could have occurred if negligence had been a factor in the incident.

The Duty Holder's Legal Defence

1. Documented Compliance: The company's comprehensive documentation of fire risk assessments, safety measures implementation, and regular training sessions provided a strong legal defence, demonstrating their commitment to safety.

2. Proactive Approach: The company's proactive approach to fire safety and learning from past incidents underscored their responsible management practices.

Conclusion

7. The incident at their site serves as a poignant reminder of the importance of thorough fire risk assessments and adherence to fire safety regulations. It highlights how a proactive approach to fire safety not only saves lives and minimises property damage but also protects against legal and financial repercussions. This case study underscores the value of learning from past incidents, continuous improvement in safety practices, and the critical role of duty holders in maintaining fire safety standards.

Chapter 18:

The Path to Safer Workplaces: The

Role of the Duty Holder

The path to safer workplaces in the realm of fire safety and general occupational health and safety is significantly influenced by the role of the duty holder. The duty holder, often defined by various health and safety legislations, is typically the employer or any person who has control over a workplace or site. Their role is pivotal in establishing, maintaining, and continuously improving the safety standards of the workplace. Here's an overview of how the duty holder contributes to creating safer workplaces:

Understanding the Role of the Duty Holder

1. Responsibility for Safety: The duty holder is legally responsible for ensuring the safety and health of employees and any other individuals who might be affected by the workplace activities.

2. Risk Assessment: A key responsibility is conducting thorough risk assessments to identify potential hazards and risks in the workplace, including fire risks, and taking appropriate measures to mitigate them.

3. Implementing Safety Measures: Based on the risk assessment, the duty holder must implement necessary safety measures. This includes providing adequate fire

safety equipment, ensuring safe work practices, and maintaining safe working conditions.

4. Training and Information: Providing appropriate training and information to all employees regarding health and safety risks and the measures in place to protect them is crucial.

The Path to Safer Workplaces

1. Developing Safety Policies: Creating and implementing comprehensive safety policies that cover all aspects of workplace safety, from fire safety protocols to emergency response procedures.

2. Cultivating a Safety Culture: Encouraging a culture of safety in the workplace where employees are proactive about safety issues, report potential hazards, and participate in safety training enthusiastically.

3. Continuous Monitoring and Improvement: Regularly monitoring safety measures for their effectiveness and making improvements wherever necessary.

4. Legal Compliance: Ensuring compliance with all relevant health and safety legislation, which can include fire safety regulations, occupational health standards, and more.

5. Employee Engagement and Feedback: Engaging with employees to get feedback on safety measures and incorporating their suggestions into safety planning.

Challenges and Solutions

1. Balancing Productivity and Safety: Finding a balance between maintaining high productivity and ensuring robust safety practices can be challenging. Effective communication and employee involvement can help in addressing this challenge.

2. Keeping Up with Changes: Staying updated with the latest regulations, technological advancements, and industry best practices requires a commitment to continuous learning and adaptation.

The duty holder plays a critical role in paving the path to safer workplaces. Through diligent risk management, implementation of effective safety measures, fostering a culture of safety, and ensuring compliance with legal standards, they can significantly reduce the risks associated with workplace activities. This proactive approach not only safeguards employees but also contributes to the overall success and sustainability of the organisation.

Chapter 19:

Staying Updated with Evolving

Regulations and Standards

Staying updated with evolving regulations and standards is essential for organisations to ensure compliance, maintain safety, and minimise legal and financial risks. This is particularly important in areas such as workplace safety, environmental regulations, and industry-specific standards. Here's an overview of how organisations can stay abreast of these changes:

Understanding the Importance

1. Legal Compliance: Laws and regulations often change, and non-compliance can lead to fines, legal action, and reputational damage.

2. Safety and Efficiency: Updated regulations often reflect new research and technological advancements, which can improve safety and operational efficiency.

3. Competitive Advantage: Staying informed about changes can provide a competitive edge by enabling proactive adaptation to new requirements.

Strategies for Staying Updated

1. Subscriptions to Regulatory Bodies: Regularly subscribe to newsletters or updates from relevant regulatory bodies or government agencies. This ensures direct

receipt of information on new regulations or changes to existing ones.

2. Industry Associations and Groups: Participate in industry associations or professional groups, which often provide resources and updates on industry-specific regulations and standards.

3. Training and Continuing Education: Encourage or mandate ongoing training and professional development for employees, particularly those in compliance and management roles. This helps in keeping staff informed about current best practices and regulatory requirements.

4. Consultation with Legal and Industry Experts: Regular consultations with legal experts or industry consultants can provide insights into regulatory trends and compliance strategies.

5. Attending Seminars and Conferences: These events are valuable sources of information about emerging trends, regulatory changes, and industry best practices.

6. Implementing a Compliance Management System: Such systems can track regulatory changes and manage compliance tasks, ensuring that the organisation adapts to changes in regulations.

Challenges

- Volume and Complexity of Information: Regulatory landscapes can be complex and vast, making it challenging to keep track of every change.

- Resource Constraints: Smaller organisations might struggle with dedicating sufficient resources to stay updated.

- Global Operations: For businesses operating in multiple jurisdictions, staying compliant with varying international regulations can be particularly challenging.

Solutions

- Dedicated Compliance Team: Establishing a team dedicated to compliance can centralise efforts to monitor and implement regulatory changes.

- Technology Utilisation: Leveraging technology like compliance management software can streamline the process of tracking and adapting to regulatory changes.

- Regular Internal Reviews: Conducting regular internal audits and reviews can help in identifying areas where updates or changes are needed in response to new regulations.

Staying updated with evolving regulations and standards is a dynamic and continuous process that requires a dedicated effort from organisations. By utilising a mix of strategies including leveraging technology, engaging in industry networks, and continuous education, organisations can effectively stay compliant, enhance their operational safety, and maintain a competitive edge in their industry.

Chapter 20:

Fire Compartmentation in the UK

Fire compartmentation is a vital aspect of fire prevention and safety in building design. It involves dividing a building into multiple compartments or sections using fire-resistant materials. These compartments are designed to contain a fire in the area where it starts, preventing or slowing its spread to other parts of the building. This method is crucial for providing occupants more time to evacuate safely and limiting property damage.

Key elements of fire compartmentation include fire-resistant walls, floors, doors, and dampers, which are built to withstand fire for a specified period, typically ranging from 30 minutes to several hours.

Why Fire Compartmentation Is Needed

- Life Safety: Primarily, it's about protecting people. Fire compartmentation gives occupants more time to escape and reduces the risk of injury or fatalities.

- Property Protection: By containing a fire, it minimises damage to other parts of a building, saving repair costs.

- Legal Compliance: Adhering to building and fire safety regulations, which often require fire compartmentation in certain types of buildings.

- Insurance Requirements: Meeting the criteria set by insurance companies for fire safety.

When Fire Compartmentation Surveys Are Needed

- New Construction: During the design and construction of new buildings to ensure compliance with fire safety standards.

- Building Renovations: When modifying existing structures, especially if changes might affect the integrity of existing fire compartmentation.

- Post-Fire Incident: After a fire, to assess and restore the fire compartmentation system.

- Regular Compliance Checks: As part of ongoing building maintenance and safety checks.

How Fire Compartmentation Surveys Are Carried Out

- Visual Inspections: Surveyors conduct thorough inspections of the building, examining walls, floors, ceilings, doors, and other elements that contribute to fire compartmentation.

- Identifying Breaches: Detecting any breaches or weaknesses in compartmentation, such as gaps or voids in walls, ceilings, or around service penetrations.

- Assessing Fire Doors: Checking the integrity and functionality of fire doors, including seals, hinges, and closing mechanisms.

- Documentation: Creating detailed reports that document the current state of fire compartmentation, highlighting any issues or areas for improvement.

Choosing a Competent Surveyor

- Certification and Experience: Look for surveyors with specific certifications in fire safety and experience in conducting fire compartmentation surveys.

- Knowledge of Regulations: Ensure they have a thorough understanding of UK building and fire safety regulations.

- Reputation and Reviews: Check their reputation in the industry, customer reviews, and references.

- Comprehensive Approach: Choose someone who offers a detailed and thorough approach to surveying, including providing clear, actionable recommendations.

Fire compartmentation and its surveys are integral to maintaining robust fire safety standards in buildings. They play a key role in safeguarding lives and properties from the devastation of fire. Regular surveys by competent professionals ensure that buildings not only comply with legal requirements but also provide a safer environment for their occupants.

Chapter 21:

Fire Door Inspections for Safety

Fire door inspections in the UK are critical assessments designed to ensure that fire doors in a building function correctly and meet safety standards. Given the vital role of fire doors in preventing the spread of fire and smoke, ensuring their proper installation and maintenance is essential for the safety of building occupants.

Importance of Fire Door Inspections

- Life Safety: The primary function of fire doors is to save lives by containing fire and smoke, thereby providing occupants more time to evacuate safely.

- Legal Compliance: UK fire safety regulations require fire doors to be correctly installed and maintained in buildings, particularly in commercial and multi-occupancy residential settings.

- Insurance Requirements: Compliance with fire safety regulations, including the maintenance of fire doors, is often a prerequisite for insurance coverage.

- Property Protection: Effective fire doors can significantly reduce property damage during a fire incident.

When Fire Door Inspections Are Required

- Post-Installation: After the installation of fire doors, to ensure they meet the required standards.

- Regular Maintenance Checks: Routine inspections are necessary to maintain the functionality and compliance of fire doors over time.

- Following Alterations or Repairs: Any time a fire door is altered or repaired, an inspection should follow to ensure compliance.

- After a Fire Incident: Inspecting fire doors after a fire to assess damage and determine if replacements or repairs are needed.

How Fire Door Inspections Are Conducted

- Physical Examination: Inspectors perform a detailed physical examination of fire doors, checking for any signs of damage or wear that could impact functionality.

- Operational Testing: Testing the operation of the door, including self-closing mechanisms, locks, and latches.

- Integrity of Seals: Checking the integrity of intumescent seals and smoke seals, which are crucial for the door's performance in a fire.

- Compliance with Standards: Ensuring the fire door and its components meet the current UK fire safety standards.

- Documentation and Reporting: Providing a detailed report on each fire door, outlining any deficiencies and recommending corrective actions.

Choosing a Competent Inspector

- Experience and Expertise: Experienced inspectors with a deep understanding of fire door standards and regulations are essential.

- Reputation and Reliability: Consider the inspector's reputation in the industry, including feedback from previous clients.

- Detailed Reporting: Ensure that the inspector provides comprehensive reports that clearly outline any issues and necessary actions.

Regular fire door inspections are a crucial aspect of fire safety management in buildings. These inspections not only ensure compliance with fire safety regulations but also play a significant role in protecting lives and property in the event of a fire. Selecting a qualified and experienced inspector is key to ensuring that fire doors in a building are fit for purpose and comply with all relevant safety standards.

A Final Word to Readers

The authors have taken utmost pains in researching and presenting the contents within this title. However, we are aware that with time newer practices and legal guidelines could make the facts and ideas presented here obsolete. We request readers to keep checking the HSE online portal and other resources listed and in the references section below to ensure that their knowledge about the issues and the legalities remain up-to-date and so that they are clear about how to proceed with fire safety and management in the best practicable way.

About The Authors

Neil Munro

I'm Neil. I thought you might like to find out a little bit about me. As of 2024 I'm 44 years old – wow, it's strange seeing that in writing, as in my head I still feel like I'm 19, although the grey hairs say something different.

I'm lucky to be married to my best mate, Eleanor. We celebrated 15 years of marriage on 11th October 2023. Together, we have been very fortunate to have two children, our son Reid and our daughter Freya.

It's great having one of each – one minute, I can be playing *Minecraft* and the next, I'm putting clothes on one of the hundreds of dolls who seem to be taking over our home.

I love eating! Whether it's eating out, take-aways, BBQs or cooking at home, I love a good meal. Whenever I look at the menu, my first thoughts are always *what's the biggest thing on here?*

Now, I know this is probably painting a bad picture of me, but, in fact, all the above is more of a treat and I take everything in moderation.

In fact, I have the most disciplined diet of anyone I know, much to the humour of my work mates. I like to keep myself fit, which does allow for some of those extra treats now and again.

I've been in the asbestos and health and safety industry since 2003 and I can't get away from it. If I'm not working around asbestos, I'm reading articles about it, writing articles about it, training people about it... I've even got pictures of it on the walls in my house.

This passion of mine has given me the knowledge and experience to help clients whatever the asbestos situation may be.

I'm a fully qualified and competent asbestos surveyor, air monitoring analyst, bulk analyst, consultant and trainer. I have worked within a number of UKAS accredited, Non UKAS accredited and asbestos removal contractor organisations. This has given me invaluable experience within all areas of the asbestos industry.

I am a Fellow member of the RSPH and hold a multitude of proficiency certificates in asbestos inspection, testing and licensed asbestos removal management. I've been an asbestos trainer for many years.

During my time working for an asbestos removal contractor, I was actively involved and instrumental in the company achieving two major milestones. Firstly, was successfully gaining

UKAS accreditation as an inspection body and secondly, was being granted a full HSE license to work with asbestos. As a new company, all quality manuals, risk assessments, controlled documents, procedural documents had to be produced, rolled out, verified and audited accordingly.

As the founding Director of Acorn Analytical Services Northampton office and Acorn Health and Safety, I've had the pleasure of helping a vast range of clients complete their projects, always on time, always within budget.

I work with clients to not only ensure that they become compliant, but more importantly that they understand what they need to do.

Ian Stone

I've written a little bit about myself, so you can get to know who's behind the book. I'm married to my wonderful wife Sian and together we have an amazing little boy called Jaxon. He's the funniest kid that either of us know – he's forever making his own jokes up and making us laugh. He's a veracious reader, and I'm really proud of him and his achievements so far.

I love all things motorcycle, especially the IOM TT and the Moto GP – what those riders do is amazing. I love to cook outside on barbecues or in wood-fired ovens and really enjoy socialising with friends and family especially in the summer.

The downside to all the fun bits that most people enjoy is that I'm an asbestos geek. I started in the asbestos industry in 2002 and have carried out all manner of jobs in the industry.

It's an affliction, as once you're in the asbestos industry it's rare that you leave, but I love it! I really enjoy assisting people to move from a place of headache to asbestos freedom.

I hold the Certificate of Competence in Asbestos and am a Fellow member of the Royal Society for Public Health. I also hold several proficiency module qualifications in asbestos and occupational hygiene. With these qualifications, you can be safe in the knowledge that the advice you receive is that of a proven expert.

My asbestos career has been slightly more eclectic than most, which has helped provide such an overview of the asbestos industry and issues surrounding asbestos management.

I am a qualified and competent surveyor, air analyst, bulk analyst and consultant who has worked within both UKAS and Non UKAS organisations.

As well as working on the asbestos consultancy side of the industry, I have also worked on the asbestos removal contracting side by helping a business obtain their 1-year and then 3-year asbestos removal licence.

For over three years, I left day-to-day practice to become the Manager of ATaC, the leading asbestos trade association for Asbestos Testing and Consulting businesses in the UK. During my time, I helped develop new asbestos industry qualifications through the RSPH (Royal Society for Public Health).

Whilst at ATaC, I also lobbied Parliament, working with the Asbestos in Schools steering group, which was at the time headed up by Michael Lees MBE. Michael was honoured by the Queen for the amazing work he had completed following the death of his wife 13 years previous from mesothelioma.

After working together for a number of years, I approached several MPs to write letters of support along with an application for Michael to be honoured. Michael was subsequently honoured with an MBE on the Queen's birthday honours list as a Campaigner and Founder of Asbestos in Schools Group for services to the Wellbeing of Children and Teachers.

I re-joined practice after ATaC and I am now a Director of Acorn Analytical Services and Acorn Safety Services, which are asbestos and health and safety consultancies respectively. I assist with the running of the business as well as providing impartial and practical consultancy advice to businesses.

Appendix

Fire Risk Assessment Checklist

Creating a Fire Risk Assessment Checklist is an essential step in identifying potential fire hazards in a workplace or building and implementing measures to mitigate these risks.

Over the next few pages we have provided a basic checklist that can be used to understand how assessments are conducted.

The checklist can be used to work through and ensure that you understand and have everything fully in place / as a starting point to help become compliant.

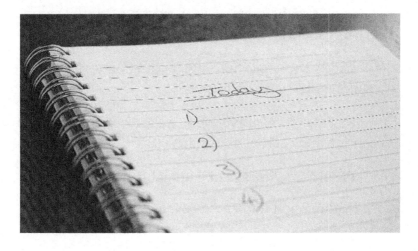

Fire Risk Assessment Checklist

1. Identify Fire Hazards

- ☐ Sources of Ignition (e.g., electrical equipment, heating appliances, open flames)

- ☐ Combustible Materials (e.g., paper, textiles, wood)

- ☐ Flammable Substances (e.g., solvents, gases, chemicals)

2. Identify People at Risk

- ☐ Employees, visitors, and customers in the premises

- ☐ Individuals in close proximity to fire hazards

- ☐ Persons with mobility or sensory impairments

- ☐ Remote or isolated workers

3. Evaluate, Remove or Reduce Risks

- ☐ Assess the likelihood of a fire starting

- ☐ Evaluate the adequacy of existing fire detection and alarm systems

- ☐ Check the condition and accessibility of firefighting equipment (e.g., extinguishers)

- ☐ Review fire prevention measures for sources of ignition and combustible materials

- ☐ Ensure safe storage of flammable materials

4. Record Findings and Implement Them

- ☐ Document hazards identified and actions taken

- ☐ Create an action plan for unresolved issues

- ☐ Inform and instruct relevant people about risks and measures implemented

5. Review and Update the Assessment

- ☐ Schedule regular reviews of the fire risk assessment

- ☐ Update the assessment in case of significant changes in the workplace

- ☐ Amend emergency plans and training as necessary

6. Emergency Routes and Exits

- ☐ Check that all escape routes are clear and well-marked

- ☐ Ensure that all fire doors are operational and not obstructed

- ☐ Verify that emergency lighting is working

7. Fire Detection and Warning Systems

- ☐ Test fire alarms and detection systems regularly

- ☐ Ensure that alarm systems are audible throughout the entire premises

8. Training and Drills

- ☐ Provide regular fire safety training to all staff

- ☐ Conduct fire drills periodically

- ☐ Train selected staff in the use of firefighting equipment

9. Firefighting Equipment

- ☐ Ensure the appropriate type and number of fire extinguishers are available

- ☐ Regularly inspect and maintain all firefighting equipment

10. Special Considerations

- ☐ Assess any particular risks related to the nature of the business or building

- ☐ Consider the need for specific measures for vulnerable persons

11. Signage and Notices

- ☐ Display appropriate fire action notices and signs

- ☐ Mark all fire equipment and exits clearly

12. Cooperation and Coordination

- ☐ Coordinate fire safety practices with other businesses in shared buildings

- ☐ Share relevant fire safety information with all occupants

This checklist provides a foundational framework for conducting a fire risk assessment. It's important to adapt and expand this checklist to suit the specific characteristics of the building and the nature of activities conducted within it. Regular review and updating of the fire risk assessment are essential to ensure ongoing safety and compliance with fire safety regulations.

Fire Door Inspection Checklist

Creating a Fire Door Inspection Checklist is an essential step in identifying potential fire hazards in a workplace or building and implementing measures to mitigate these risks.

Over the next few pages we have provided a basic checklist that can be used to understand how assessments are conducted.

The checklist can be used to work through and ensure that you understand and have everything fully in place / as a starting point to help become compliant.

1. General Condition

- ☐ Check for obvious damage or wear

- ☐ Ensure the door is not warped or distorted

2. Door Leaf and Frame

- ☐ Confirm the door leaf is securely attached to the frame

- ☐ Ensure no gaps larger than 4mm between door and frame

3. Integrity of Seals

- ☐ Inspect intumescent seals for damage or absence

- ☐ Check smoke seals for damage and proper operation

4. Hinges

- ☐ Verify there are at least three hinges in good condition

- ☐ Ensure hinges are securely fixed and not loose

5. Door Closer and Openers

- ☐ Check door closer is properly adjusted and functional

- ☐ Ensure the door fully closes from any open position

6. Locks and Latches

- □ Ensure locks and latches operate smoothly

- □ Check for proper engagement with the door frame

7. Glazing in Door

- □ Check for cracked or broken glass

- □ Ensure glazing beads are intact and secure

8. Gaps and Threshold

- □ Verify gap under the door is consistent and not excessive

- □ Check the threshold for damage or wear

9. Signage

- □ Ensure fire door signage is present and legible

10. Overall Operation

- □ Test the door's overall operation for smoothness and ease

This checklist provides a basic framework and should be adapted as necessary. Regular inspections are crucial for ensuring the effectiveness and compliance of fire doors.

Useful Resources and Websites

Consultancy and Assistance

1. Acorn Safety Services Ltd

    (www.acornhealthandsafety.co.uk/what-we-do/fire-risk-assessments): Offers consultancy services and guidance on fire safety responsibilities and risk assessments in the workplace, specific to UK regulations. Acorn are members of The Institute of Fire Safety Managers.

Fire Safety and Risk Assessment Guidance

2. UK Government Fire Safety Guidance

    (www.gov.uk/workplace-fire-safety-your-responsibilities): Offers official guidance on fire safety responsibilities and risk assessments in the workplace, specific to UK regulations.

3. National Fire Protection Association (NFPA)

    (www.nfpa.org): Provides a wealth of resources on fire safety standards, codes, and research, including materials on risk assessments.

4. The Institution of Fire Engineers (IFE)

    (www.ife.org.uk): Offers resources and guidance for fire engineering professionals, including aspects of fire risk assessment.

5. Health and Safety Executive (HSE) – Fire Safety

(www.hse.gov.uk/toolbox/fire.htm): Provides practical advice and guidance on fire safety and risk management in the workplace.

Educational and Training Resources

1. Fire Service College

   (www.fireservicecollege.ac.uk): Offers training and qualifications in various aspects of fire safety, including risk assessment.

2. Fire Protection Association (FPA)

   (www.thefpa.co.uk): Offers training, advice, and resources on fire risk assessment and fire protection.

Forums and Community Groups

1. UK Fire Service Forum

   (www.fireservice.co.uk/forum): A forum for discussing various aspects of fire safety, including risk assessments.

Glossary of Terms

1. Fire Risk Assessment (FRA): A systematic process to evaluate the potential risks that might lead to a fire in a building or premises, aiming to identify fire hazards and determine who might be in danger.

2. Duty Holder: The individual or entity responsible for conducting the FRA, often the employer, landlord, or owner of the premises.

3. Fire Hazard: Any condition, substance, or activity that potentially can cause a fire or contribute to its severity.

4. Ignition Source: An item or circumstance that can initiate a fire, such as electrical equipment, heaters, or open flames.

5. Fuel Load: The amount and type of materials in an area that can burn and contribute to a fire's intensity.

6. Combustibles: Materials that can ignite and burn, including items like paper, wood, fabrics, and certain types of plastics.

7. Flammable Liquids/Gases: Substances that can easily ignite, including solvents, fuels, and aerosols.

8. Fire Resistance: The ability of a material or assembly to withstand fire or give protection from it.

9. Fire Suppression Systems: Systems such as sprinklers and fire extinguishers designed to extinguish or control fires.

10. Means of Egress: A continuous and unobstructed path of exit from any point in a building or structure to a safe place (outside).

11. Fire Detection Systems: Systems designed to detect and alert the presence of fire, smoke, or heat, including smoke detectors and heat sensors.

12. NFPA (National Fire Protection Association): An international organisation that develops and publishes fire protection and safety standards.

13. Evacuation Plan: A strategy for the safe exit of people from a building or area in case of fire or other emergencies.

14. Fire Safety Audit: A systematic examination of a building's fire safety management systems and processes.

15. Hot Work: Any work that involves burning, welding, or using fire- or spark-producing tools.

16. Passive Fire Protection (PFP): Building design aspects that inherently provide fire resistance, such as fire doors and fire-resistant wall assemblies.

17. Active Fire Protection (AFP): Systems that require some degree of motion and response to work, like fire sprinkler systems.

18. Emergency Lighting: Lighting that automatically operates when the power supply to the normal lighting fails, ensuring visibility in escape routes.

19. BS 5839: British Standard for fire detection and fire alarm systems for buildings.

20. Fire Drill: A practice of the emergency procedures to be used in case of fire.

21. Compartmentation: Dividing a building into smaller sections to prevent or slow the spread of fire.

22. RRFSO (Regulatory Reform (Fire Safety) Order 2005): UK legislation focusing on fire safety in non-domestic premises.

Are You Still Looking to Remove Your Fire Risk?

Do you want help instead of going it alone?

Claim Your Complimentary <u>Audit</u>* Worth

£697.00

Are you sure you're legally compliant?

Go here now and claim:

www.acornhealthandsafety.co.uk/what-we-do/fire-risk-assessments/
In the "How Can we Help You" Box type "Book Audit"

For a limited time, we're offering you a 20-minute strategy session where we'll discuss your business goals and challenges and draw up a H&S Blueprint for you for free.

*Please note this is NOT a sales call. You will be speaking with one of our highly experienced Consultants, not a salesperson.

Other titles available from Amazon:

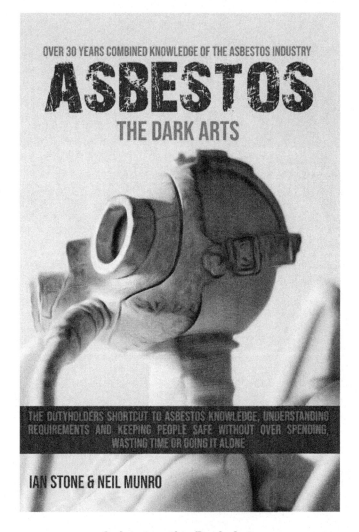

Asbestos the Dark Arts

The Dutyholder's' Shortcut to Asbestos Knowledge

Understanding Requirements and Keeping People Safe Without Overspending, Wasting Time or Going it Alone

Other titles available from Amazon:

Fear and Loathing of
Health and Safety

Stay out of prison, avoid massive fines, and cut through the red tape

Other titles available from Amazon:

Legionella the Dark Arts

The Dutyholders' Shortcut to Legionella Knowledge

Understanding Requirements and Keeping People Safe Without Overspending, Wasting Time or Going it Alone

Printed in Great Britain
by Amazon

36853189R00086